50 Classic Cake Recipes for Every Occasion

By: Kelly Johnson

Table of Contents

- Classic Vanilla Cake
- Chocolate Fudge Cake
- Red Velvet Cake
- Carrot Cake
- Lemon Drizzle Cake
- Black Forest Cake
- German Chocolate Cake
- Classic Pound Cake
- Funfetti Birthday Cake
- Tres Leches Cake
- Coconut Cake
- Hummingbird Cake
- Strawberry Shortcake
- Angel Food Cake
- Devil's Food Cake
- Boston Cream Pie
- Opera Cake
- Flourless Chocolate Cake
- Victoria Sponge Cake
- Italian Ricotta Cake
- Pineapple Upside-Down Cake
- Tiramisu Cake
- Classic Cheesecake
- Coffee Walnut Cake
- Peanut Butter Cake
- Butter Pecan Cake
- Gingerbread Cake
- Molten Lava Cake
- White Chocolate Raspberry Cake
- Chiffon Cake
- Orange Olive Oil Cake
- Blackberry Almond Cake
- Banana Cake with Cream Cheese Frosting
- Cherry Almond Cake
- Matcha Green Tea Cake

- Pumpkin Spice Cake
- Raspberry Lemon Cake
- Funfetti Bundt Cake
- Maple Walnut Cake
- Chocolate Marble Cake
- Honey Cake
- Spice Cake with Brown Butter Frosting
- Mocha Layer Cake
- Almond Amaretto Cake
- Sour Cream Coffee Cake
- Coconut Tres Leches Cake
- Sticky Toffee Pudding Cake
- Chocolate Peanut Butter Cake
- Apple Cinnamon Cake
- Chocolate Swiss Roll Cake

Classic Vanilla Cake

Ingredients:

- 2 ½ cups (315g) all-purpose flour
- 2 ½ teaspoons baking powder
- ½ teaspoon salt
- 1 cup (226g) unsalted butter, softened
- 1 ¾ cups (350g) sugar
- 4 eggs
- 1 tablespoon vanilla extract
- 1 cup (240ml) whole milk

Instructions:

1. Preheat oven to 350°F (175°C). Grease and flour two 9-inch cake pans.
2. Whisk flour, baking powder, and salt.
3. Beat butter and sugar until fluffy. Add eggs one at a time, then mix in vanilla.
4. Alternate adding dry ingredients and milk.
5. Bake for 30-35 minutes. Cool before frosting.

Chocolate Fudge Cake

Ingredients:

- 2 cups (250g) all-purpose flour
- ¾ cup (75g) cocoa powder
- 2 teaspoons baking powder
- 1 teaspoon baking soda
- ½ teaspoon salt
- 1 cup (226g) butter, softened
- 1 ¾ cups (350g) sugar
- 3 eggs
- 1 teaspoon vanilla extract
- 1 cup (240ml) buttermilk
- ½ cup (120ml) hot coffee

Instructions:

1. Preheat oven to 350°F (175°C). Grease two 9-inch cake pans.
2. Whisk flour, cocoa, baking powder, soda, and salt.
3. Beat butter and sugar until fluffy. Add eggs one at a time, then mix in vanilla.
4. Alternate adding dry ingredients with buttermilk. Stir in hot coffee.
5. Bake for 30-35 minutes. Cool before frosting.

Red Velvet Cake

Ingredients:

- 2 ½ cups (315g) all-purpose flour
- 1 teaspoon baking soda
- 1 teaspoon salt
- 2 tablespoons cocoa powder
- 1 cup (226g) butter, softened
- 1 ¾ cups (350g) sugar
- 2 eggs
- 1 tablespoon vanilla extract
- 1 tablespoon red food coloring
- 1 cup (240ml) buttermilk
- 1 teaspoon vinegar

Instructions:

1. Preheat oven to 350°F (175°C). Grease two 9-inch cake pans.
2. Whisk flour, baking soda, salt, and cocoa.
3. Beat butter and sugar, add eggs, vanilla, and food coloring.
4. Alternate adding dry ingredients with buttermilk, then mix in vinegar.
5. Bake for 30-35 minutes. Cool before frosting with cream cheese frosting.

Carrot Cake

Ingredients:

- 2 cups (250g) all-purpose flour
- 2 teaspoons baking powder
- 1 teaspoon baking soda
- 1 teaspoon cinnamon
- ½ teaspoon nutmeg
- ½ teaspoon salt
- 1 cup (200g) sugar
- ¾ cup (180ml) vegetable oil
- 3 eggs
- 1 teaspoon vanilla extract
- 2 cups (220g) grated carrots
- ½ cup (60g) chopped walnuts (optional)

Instructions:

1. Preheat oven to 350°F (175°C). Grease two 9-inch cake pans.
2. Whisk flour, baking powder, soda, cinnamon, nutmeg, and salt.
3. Beat sugar, oil, eggs, and vanilla. Stir in carrots and walnuts.
4. Add dry ingredients and mix.
5. Bake for 30-35 minutes. Cool before frosting with cream cheese frosting.

Lemon Drizzle Cake

Ingredients:

- 1 cup (226g) butter, softened
- 1 cup (200g) sugar
- 3 eggs
- 1 ½ cups (190g) all-purpose flour
- 1 teaspoon baking powder
- ¼ teaspoon salt
- Zest of 2 lemons
- ½ cup (120ml) milk

For the drizzle:

- ¼ cup (60ml) lemon juice
- ½ cup (100g) sugar

Instructions:

1. Preheat oven to 350°F (175°C). Grease a loaf pan.
2. Beat butter and sugar. Add eggs, one at a time.
3. Mix in flour, baking powder, salt, zest, and milk.
4. Bake for 40-45 minutes.
5. Mix lemon juice and sugar. Pour over warm cake.

Black Forest Cake

Ingredients:

- 1 ¾ cups (220g) all-purpose flour
- ¾ cup (75g) cocoa powder
- 2 teaspoons baking powder
- ½ teaspoon salt
- 1 cup (200g) sugar
- ¾ cup (180ml) vegetable oil
- 3 eggs
- 1 teaspoon vanilla extract
- ¾ cup (180ml) buttermilk
- 1 cup (200g) cherries, pitted

Instructions:

1. Preheat oven to 350°F (175°C). Grease two 9-inch cake pans.
2. Whisk flour, cocoa, baking powder, and salt.
3. Beat sugar, oil, eggs, and vanilla. Add dry ingredients, then buttermilk.
4. Fold in cherries. Bake for 30-35 minutes.
5. Fill with whipped cream and cherries.

German Chocolate Cake

Ingredients:

- 2 cups (250g) all-purpose flour
- ¾ cup (75g) cocoa powder
- 1 teaspoon baking powder
- 1 teaspoon baking soda
- ½ teaspoon salt
- 1 cup (200g) sugar
- ¾ cup (180ml) vegetable oil
- 3 eggs
- 1 teaspoon vanilla extract
- 1 cup (240ml) buttermilk

For the frosting:

- 1 cup (200g) sugar
- ½ cup (120ml) evaporated milk
- ½ cup (113g) butter
- 3 egg yolks
- 1 cup (100g) shredded coconut
- ½ cup (60g) chopped pecans

Instructions:

1. Preheat oven to 350°F (175°C). Grease two 9-inch cake pans.
2. Mix dry ingredients, then beat in wet ingredients.
3. Bake for 30-35 minutes. Cool.
4. Cook frosting ingredients until thick. Stir in coconut and pecans.

Classic Pound Cake

Ingredients:

- 1 cup (226g) butter, softened
- 2 cups (400g) sugar
- 4 eggs
- 2 teaspoons vanilla extract
- 3 cups (375g) flour
- 1 teaspoon baking powder
- ½ teaspoon salt
- 1 cup (240ml) milk

Instructions:

1. Preheat oven to 350°F (175°C). Grease a loaf pan.
2. Beat butter and sugar. Add eggs and vanilla.
3. Mix dry ingredients, then add with milk.
4. Bake for 50-60 minutes.

Funfetti Birthday Cake

Ingredients:

- 2 ½ cups (315g) all-purpose flour
- 2 teaspoons baking powder
- ½ teaspoon salt
- 1 cup (226g) butter, softened
- 1 ¾ cups (350g) sugar
- 4 eggs
- 1 tablespoon vanilla extract
- 1 cup (240ml) whole milk
- ½ cup (90g) rainbow sprinkles

Instructions:

1. Preheat oven to 350°F (175°C). Grease two 9-inch cake pans.
2. Mix dry ingredients. Beat butter, sugar, eggs, and vanilla.
3. Alternate adding flour and milk. Fold in sprinkles.
4. Bake for 30-35 minutes. Cool before frosting.

Tres Leches Cake

Ingredients:

For the cake:

- 1 cup (125g) all-purpose flour
- 1 ½ teaspoons baking powder
- ¼ teaspoon salt
- 5 eggs, separated
- 1 cup (200g) sugar
- 1 teaspoon vanilla extract
- ⅓ cup (80ml) whole milk

For the milk mixture:

- 1 can (12 oz) evaporated milk
- 1 can (14 oz) sweetened condensed milk
- ½ cup (120ml) heavy cream

For the topping:

- 1 cup (240ml) heavy whipping cream
- 2 tablespoons sugar

Instructions:

1. Preheat oven to 350°F (175°C). Grease a 9x13-inch pan.
2. Whisk flour, baking powder, and salt.
3. Beat egg yolks with sugar until pale. Mix in vanilla and milk.
4. Beat egg whites until stiff, then fold into batter. Pour into pan and bake for 30 minutes.
5. Poke holes in the cake, then pour the milk mixture over it. Chill for 4+ hours.
6. Whip cream and sugar, then spread on top before serving.

Coconut Cake

Ingredients:

- 2 ½ cups (315g) all-purpose flour
- 2 ½ teaspoons baking powder
- ½ teaspoon salt
- 1 cup (226g) butter, softened
- 1 ¾ cups (350g) sugar
- 4 eggs
- 1 teaspoon vanilla extract
- 1 teaspoon coconut extract
- 1 cup (240ml) coconut milk
- 1 cup (80g) shredded coconut

Instructions:

1. Preheat oven to 350°F (175°C). Grease two 9-inch cake pans.
2. Whisk flour, baking powder, and salt.
3. Beat butter and sugar until fluffy. Add eggs one at a time, then mix in extracts.
4. Alternate adding dry ingredients and coconut milk. Fold in shredded coconut.
5. Bake for 30-35 minutes. Cool and frost with coconut buttercream.

Hummingbird Cake

Ingredients:

- 3 cups (375g) all-purpose flour
- 1 teaspoon baking soda
- 1 teaspoon cinnamon
- ½ teaspoon salt
- 1 cup (200g) sugar
- 1 cup (200g) brown sugar
- 3 eggs
- 1 cup (240ml) vegetable oil
- 1 teaspoon vanilla extract
- 2 cups (440g) mashed ripe bananas
- 1 cup (227g) crushed pineapple, drained
- 1 cup (120g) chopped pecans

Instructions:

1. Preheat oven to 350°F (175°C). Grease two 9-inch cake pans.
2. Whisk dry ingredients together.
3. Beat eggs, oil, and vanilla. Stir in bananas and pineapple.
4. Add dry ingredients and mix. Fold in pecans.
5. Bake for 30-35 minutes. Frost with cream cheese frosting.

Strawberry Shortcake

Ingredients:

For the shortcakes:

- 2 cups (250g) all-purpose flour
- ¼ cup (50g) sugar
- 1 tablespoon baking powder
- ½ teaspoon salt
- ½ cup (113g) butter, cold and cubed
- ¾ cup (180ml) heavy cream

For the filling:

- 2 cups (300g) sliced strawberries
- ¼ cup (50g) sugar
- 1 cup (240ml) whipped cream

Instructions:

1. Preheat oven to 400°F (200°C). Whisk flour, sugar, baking powder, and salt.
2. Cut in butter, then stir in heavy cream until dough forms.
3. Roll out and cut into rounds. Bake for 15 minutes.
4. Toss strawberries with sugar. Slice shortcakes, fill with strawberries and whipped cream.

Angel Food Cake

Ingredients:

- 1 cup (125g) cake flour
- 1 ½ cups (300g) sugar
- 12 egg whites
- 1 teaspoon cream of tartar
- 1 teaspoon vanilla extract
- ¼ teaspoon salt

Instructions:

1. Preheat oven to 350°F (175°C). Sift flour and ½ cup sugar together.
2. Beat egg whites, salt, and cream of tartar until soft peaks form. Gradually add remaining sugar, then vanilla.
3. Fold in flour mixture. Pour into an ungreased tube pan.
4. Bake for 35-40 minutes. Cool upside down before removing.

Devil's Food Cake

Ingredients:

- 2 cups (250g) all-purpose flour
- ¾ cup (75g) cocoa powder
- 1 ½ teaspoons baking powder
- 1 teaspoon baking soda
- ½ teaspoon salt
- 1 cup (226g) butter, softened
- 1 ¾ cups (350g) sugar
- 3 eggs
- 1 teaspoon vanilla extract
- 1 cup (240ml) buttermilk
- ½ cup (120ml) hot coffee

Instructions:

1. Preheat oven to 350°F (175°C). Grease two 9-inch cake pans.
2. Whisk dry ingredients. Beat butter and sugar, then add eggs and vanilla.
3. Alternate adding dry ingredients and buttermilk. Stir in coffee.
4. Bake for 30-35 minutes. Frost with chocolate ganache.

Boston Cream Pie

Ingredients:

For the cake:

- 1 cup (125g) all-purpose flour
- 1 teaspoon baking powder
- ¼ teaspoon salt
- 3 eggs
- 1 cup (200g) sugar
- 1 teaspoon vanilla extract
- ½ cup (120ml) whole milk
- 2 tablespoons (28g) butter, melted

For the filling:

- 1 cup (240ml) milk
- 3 egg yolks
- ¼ cup (50g) sugar
- 2 tablespoons cornstarch
- 1 teaspoon vanilla extract

For the chocolate glaze:

- ½ cup (120ml) heavy cream
- 4 oz (113g) dark chocolate, chopped

Instructions:

1. Preheat oven to 350°F (175°C). Grease an 8-inch cake pan.
2. Beat eggs and sugar until fluffy. Fold in flour, baking powder, salt, milk, and butter.
3. Bake for 30-35 minutes.
4. Cook custard ingredients until thick. Cool.
5. Heat cream, pour over chocolate, and stir to make glaze.
6. Slice cake, fill with custard, and pour chocolate glaze on top.

Opera Cake

Ingredients:

For the cake layers:

- 6 eggs
- ¾ cup (150g) sugar
- 1 cup (125g) almond flour
- ¾ cup (95g) all-purpose flour

For the coffee syrup:

- ½ cup (120ml) hot coffee
- ¼ cup (50g) sugar

For the coffee buttercream:

- 1 cup (226g) butter, softened
- 2 cups (240g) powdered sugar
- 2 tablespoons espresso

For the chocolate ganache:

- ½ cup (120ml) heavy cream
- 6 oz (170g) dark chocolate, chopped

Instructions:

1. Bake sponge layers at 375°F (190°C) for 10-12 minutes.
2. Brush layers with coffee syrup.
3. Spread buttercream between layers.
4. Pour chocolate ganache on top. Chill before serving.

Flourless Chocolate Cake

Ingredients:

- 8 oz (225g) dark chocolate, chopped
- ½ cup (113g) butter
- ¾ cup (150g) sugar
- ¼ teaspoon salt
- 1 teaspoon vanilla extract
- 3 eggs
- ½ cup (40g) cocoa powder

Instructions:

1. Preheat oven to 375°F (190°C). Grease an 8-inch cake pan and line with parchment.
2. Melt chocolate and butter together, then stir in sugar, salt, and vanilla.
3. Whisk in eggs one at a time, then fold in cocoa powder.
4. Pour into pan and bake for 25 minutes. Cool before serving.

Victoria Sponge Cake

Ingredients:

- 1 cup (226g) butter, softened
- 1 cup (200g) sugar
- 4 eggs
- 1 teaspoon vanilla extract
- 2 cups (250g) self-rising flour
- ½ cup (120ml) milk

For the filling:

- ½ cup (120g) strawberry jam
- 1 cup (240ml) whipped cream
- Powdered sugar for dusting

Instructions:

1. Preheat oven to 350°F (175°C). Grease two 8-inch cake pans.
2. Beat butter and sugar until fluffy. Add eggs one at a time, then vanilla.
3. Fold in flour and milk.
4. Divide batter between pans and bake for 25-30 minutes.
5. Cool, then spread jam and whipped cream between layers. Dust with powdered sugar.

Italian Ricotta Cake

Ingredients:

- 1 ½ cups (190g) all-purpose flour
- 1 teaspoon baking powder
- ½ teaspoon salt
- ¾ cup (170g) butter, softened
- 1 cup (200g) sugar
- 3 eggs
- 1 teaspoon vanilla extract
- 1 teaspoon lemon zest
- 1 cup (250g) ricotta cheese

Instructions:

1. Preheat oven to 350°F (175°C). Grease a 9-inch cake pan.
2. Whisk flour, baking powder, and salt.
3. Beat butter and sugar, then add eggs, vanilla, and zest.
4. Fold in ricotta and dry ingredients.
5. Bake for 40-45 minutes.

Pineapple Upside-Down Cake

Ingredients:

- ½ cup (113g) butter, melted
- ¾ cup (150g) brown sugar
- 6 pineapple rings
- 6 maraschino cherries
- 1 ½ cups (190g) all-purpose flour
- 1 teaspoon baking powder
- ½ teaspoon salt
- ¾ cup (150g) sugar
- 2 eggs
- 1 teaspoon vanilla extract
- ½ cup (120ml) milk

Instructions:

1. Preheat oven to 350°F (175°C). Grease a 9-inch cake pan.
2. Pour melted butter into the pan and sprinkle with brown sugar. Arrange pineapple and cherries.
3. Mix flour, baking powder, and salt. Beat sugar and eggs, then add vanilla and milk.
4. Pour batter over pineapple and bake for 35-40 minutes. Flip onto a plate while warm.

Tiramisu Cake

Ingredients:

For the cake:

- 1 ½ cups (190g) all-purpose flour
- 1 teaspoon baking powder
- ½ teaspoon salt
- ¾ cup (150g) sugar
- ½ cup (113g) butter, softened
- 3 eggs
- 1 teaspoon vanilla extract
- ½ cup (120ml) milk

For the soak:

- ½ cup (120ml) strong coffee
- 2 tablespoons coffee liqueur (optional)

For the frosting:

- 8 oz (225g) mascarpone cheese
- 1 cup (240ml) heavy cream
- ¼ cup (30g) powdered sugar
- Cocoa powder for dusting

Instructions:

1. Preheat oven to 350°F (175°C). Grease two 8-inch cake pans.
2. Beat butter and sugar, then add eggs and vanilla. Mix in flour, baking powder, and milk.
3. Bake for 25-30 minutes.
4. Brush coffee mixture over cake layers.
5. Whip mascarpone, cream, and sugar. Frost the cake and dust with cocoa.

Classic Cheesecake

Ingredients:

For the crust:

- 1 ½ cups (180g) graham cracker crumbs
- 6 tablespoons (85g) butter, melted

For the filling:

- 24 oz (680g) cream cheese, softened
- 1 cup (200g) sugar
- 3 eggs
- 1 teaspoon vanilla extract
- ½ cup (120ml) sour cream

Instructions:

1. Preheat oven to 325°F (160°C). Mix crust ingredients and press into a springform pan.
2. Beat cream cheese and sugar, then add eggs and vanilla. Stir in sour cream.
3. Pour into crust and bake for 50-60 minutes. Chill for 4+ hours.

Coffee Walnut Cake

Ingredients:

- 2 cups (250g) all-purpose flour
- 2 teaspoons baking powder
- ½ teaspoon salt
- ¾ cup (150g) sugar
- ½ cup (113g) butter, softened
- 2 eggs
- 1 teaspoon vanilla extract
- ½ cup (120ml) strong coffee
- ½ cup (60g) chopped walnuts

Instructions:

1. Preheat oven to 350°F (175°C). Grease an 8-inch cake pan.
2. Beat butter and sugar, then add eggs and vanilla. Mix in flour, baking powder, salt, and coffee. Fold in walnuts.
3. Bake for 30-35 minutes.

Peanut Butter Cake

Ingredients:

- 2 cups (250g) all-purpose flour
- 1 teaspoon baking powder
- ½ teaspoon salt
- ¾ cup (170g) peanut butter
- ¾ cup (150g) sugar
- 2 eggs
- 1 teaspoon vanilla extract
- 1 cup (240ml) milk

Instructions:

1. Preheat oven to 350°F (175°C). Grease a 9-inch cake pan.
2. Beat peanut butter and sugar, then add eggs and vanilla.
3. Mix in flour, baking powder, salt, and milk.
4. Bake for 30-35 minutes.

Butter Pecan Cake

Ingredients:

- 1 cup (120g) chopped pecans
- 1 cup (226g) butter, softened
- 1 ¾ cups (350g) sugar
- 4 eggs
- 1 teaspoon vanilla extract
- 2 ½ cups (315g) all-purpose flour
- 2 teaspoons baking powder
- ½ teaspoon salt
- 1 cup (240ml) buttermilk

Instructions:

1. Preheat oven to 350°F (175°C). Toast pecans for 5 minutes.
2. Beat butter and sugar, then add eggs and vanilla.
3. Mix in flour, baking powder, salt, and buttermilk. Fold in pecans.
4. Bake for 35-40 minutes.

Gingerbread Cake

Ingredients:

- 2 cups (250g) all-purpose flour
- 1 teaspoon baking soda
- ½ teaspoon salt
- 2 teaspoons cinnamon
- 1 teaspoon ginger
- ½ teaspoon nutmeg
- ¾ cup (150g) brown sugar
- ½ cup (113g) butter, melted
- 1 cup (240ml) molasses
- 1 cup (240ml) hot water

Instructions:

1. Preheat oven to 350°F (175°C). Grease a 9-inch cake pan.
2. Mix all ingredients until smooth.
3. Bake for 35-40 minutes.

Molten Lava Cake

Ingredients:

- 4 oz (113g) dark chocolate, chopped
- ½ cup (113g) butter
- ½ cup (100g) sugar
- 2 eggs
- 2 egg yolks
- ¼ cup (30g) flour

Instructions:

1. Preheat oven to 425°F (220°C). Grease four ramekins.
2. Melt chocolate and butter. Stir in sugar.
3. Whisk in eggs and yolks, then fold in flour.
4. Divide into ramekins and bake for 10-12 minutes.
5. Serve immediately with powdered sugar or ice cream.

White Chocolate Raspberry Cake

Ingredients:

- 2 ½ cups (315g) all-purpose flour
- 2 teaspoons baking powder
- ½ teaspoon salt
- ¾ cup (170g) butter, softened
- 1 ¾ cups (350g) sugar
- 4 eggs
- 1 teaspoon vanilla extract
- 1 cup (240ml) milk
- ½ cup (90g) white chocolate chips
- 1 cup (150g) raspberries

Instructions:

1. Preheat oven to 350°F (175°C). Grease two 9-inch cake pans.
2. Whisk dry ingredients. Beat butter and sugar, add eggs and vanilla.
3. Mix in flour and milk. Fold in chocolate and raspberries.
4. Bake for 30-35 minutes.

Chiffon Cake

Ingredients:

- 2 ¼ cups (280g) cake flour
- 1 ½ cups (300g) sugar
- 1 tablespoon baking powder
- ½ teaspoon salt
- ½ cup (120ml) vegetable oil
- 7 eggs, separated
- ¾ cup (180ml) water
- 1 teaspoon vanilla extract
- ½ teaspoon cream of tartar

Instructions:

1. Preheat oven to 325°F (160°C). Grease a tube pan.
2. Mix flour, sugar, baking powder, and salt. Stir in oil, yolks, water, and vanilla.
3. Beat egg whites with cream of tartar until stiff peaks form.
4. Fold whites into batter. Bake for 50-55 minutes.

Orange Olive Oil Cake

Ingredients:

- 2 cups (250g) all-purpose flour
- 1 teaspoon baking powder
- ½ teaspoon salt
- ¾ cup (180ml) olive oil
- 1 cup (200g) sugar
- 3 eggs
- 1 teaspoon vanilla extract
- Zest and juice of 2 oranges

Instructions:

1. Preheat oven to 350°F (175°C). Grease a 9-inch cake pan.
2. Beat olive oil and sugar, add eggs, vanilla, and orange zest/juice.
3. Fold in flour, baking powder, and salt.
4. Bake for 35-40 minutes.

Blackberry Almond Cake

Ingredients:

- 1 ½ cups (190g) all-purpose flour
- 1 cup (100g) almond flour
- 1 teaspoon baking powder
- ½ teaspoon salt
- ¾ cup (170g) butter, softened
- 1 ½ cups (300g) sugar
- 3 eggs
- 1 teaspoon almond extract
- 1 cup (150g) blackberries

Instructions:

1. Preheat oven to 350°F (175°C). Grease an 8-inch cake pan.
2. Beat butter and sugar, add eggs and almond extract.
3. Mix in dry ingredients, then fold in blackberries.
4. Bake for 35-40 minutes.

Banana Cake with Cream Cheese Frosting

Ingredients:

- 2 cups (250g) all-purpose flour
- 1 teaspoon baking powder
- ½ teaspoon salt
- ¾ cup (170g) butter, softened
- 1 ½ cups (300g) sugar
- 2 eggs
- 1 teaspoon vanilla extract
- 2 cups (440g) mashed bananas
- ½ cup (120ml) milk

Instructions:

1. Preheat oven to 350°F (175°C). Grease two 9-inch cake pans.
2. Beat butter and sugar, add eggs and vanilla.
3. Mix in bananas, flour, baking powder, salt, and milk.
4. Bake for 30-35 minutes. Frost with cream cheese frosting.

Cherry Almond Cake

Ingredients:

- 2 cups (250g) all-purpose flour
- 1 teaspoon baking powder
- ½ teaspoon salt
- ¾ cup (170g) butter, softened
- 1 ½ cups (300g) sugar
- 3 eggs
- 1 teaspoon almond extract
- 1 cup (150g) cherries, pitted

Instructions:

1. Preheat oven to 350°F (175°C). Grease a 9-inch cake pan.
2. Beat butter and sugar, add eggs and almond extract.
3. Mix in dry ingredients, then fold in cherries.
4. Bake for 35-40 minutes.

Matcha Green Tea Cake

Ingredients:

- 2 cups (250g) all-purpose flour
- 1 teaspoon baking powder
- ½ teaspoon salt
- 2 tablespoons matcha powder
- ¾ cup (170g) butter, softened
- 1 ½ cups (300g) sugar
- 3 eggs
- 1 teaspoon vanilla extract
- 1 cup (240ml) milk

Instructions:

1. Preheat oven to 350°F (175°C). Grease a 9-inch cake pan.
2. Beat butter and sugar, add eggs and vanilla.
3. Mix in flour, matcha, baking powder, salt, and milk.
4. Bake for 30-35 minutes.

Pumpkin Spice Cake

Ingredients:

- 2 cups (250g) all-purpose flour
- 1 teaspoon baking soda
- 1 teaspoon cinnamon
- ½ teaspoon nutmeg
- ½ teaspoon ginger
- ½ teaspoon salt
- ¾ cup (170g) butter, softened
- 1 ½ cups (300g) sugar
- 2 eggs
- 1 teaspoon vanilla extract
- 1 cup (225g) pumpkin puree

Instructions:

1. Preheat oven to 350°F (175°C). Grease a 9-inch cake pan.
2. Beat butter and sugar, add eggs and vanilla.
3. Mix in dry ingredients and pumpkin puree.
4. Bake for 35-40 minutes.

Raspberry Lemon Cake

Ingredients:

- 2 cups (250g) all-purpose flour
- 1 teaspoon baking powder
- ½ teaspoon salt
- Zest of 2 lemons
- ¾ cup (170g) butter, softened
- 1 ½ cups (300g) sugar
- 3 eggs
- 1 teaspoon vanilla extract
- ½ cup (120ml) lemon juice
- 1 cup (150g) raspberries

Instructions:

1. Preheat oven to 350°F (175°C). Grease a 9-inch cake pan.
2. Beat butter and sugar, add eggs and vanilla.
3. Mix in dry ingredients, lemon juice, and zest. Fold in raspberries.
4. Bake for 35-40 minutes.

Funfetti Bundt Cake

Ingredients:

- 2 ½ cups (315g) all-purpose flour
- 1 teaspoon baking powder
- ½ teaspoon salt
- ¾ cup (170g) butter, softened
- 1 ¾ cups (350g) sugar
- 4 eggs
- 1 teaspoon vanilla extract
- 1 cup (240ml) milk
- ½ cup (90g) rainbow sprinkles

Instructions:

1. Preheat oven to 350°F (175°C). Grease a bundt pan.
2. Beat butter and sugar, add eggs and vanilla.
3. Mix in dry ingredients and milk. Fold in sprinkles.
4. Bake for 40-45 minutes.

Maple Walnut Cake

Ingredients:

- 2 ½ cups (315g) all-purpose flour
- 2 teaspoons baking powder
- ½ teaspoon salt
- ¾ cup (170g) butter, softened
- 1 cup (200g) brown sugar
- ½ cup (120ml) maple syrup
- 3 eggs
- 1 teaspoon vanilla extract
- 1 cup (240ml) buttermilk
- 1 cup (120g) chopped walnuts

Instructions:

1. Preheat oven to 350°F (175°C). Grease two 9-inch cake pans.
2. Beat butter and sugar, then add maple syrup, eggs, and vanilla.
3. Mix in flour, baking powder, salt, and buttermilk. Fold in walnuts.
4. Bake for 30-35 minutes. Frost with maple buttercream.

Chocolate Marble Cake

Ingredients:

- 2 ½ cups (315g) all-purpose flour
- 2 teaspoons baking powder
- ½ teaspoon salt
- ¾ cup (170g) butter, softened
- 1 ¾ cups (350g) sugar
- 4 eggs
- 1 teaspoon vanilla extract
- 1 cup (240ml) milk
- ¼ cup (30g) cocoa powder
- 2 tablespoons hot water

Instructions:

1. Preheat oven to 350°F (175°C). Grease a bundt pan.
2. Beat butter and sugar, then add eggs and vanilla.
3. Mix in flour, baking powder, salt, and milk.
4. Divide batter in half. Mix cocoa and hot water into one half.
5. Alternate spoonfuls of vanilla and chocolate batter into the pan and swirl with a knife.
6. Bake for 40-45 minutes.

Honey Cake

Ingredients:

- 2 ½ cups (315g) all-purpose flour
- 1 teaspoon baking powder
- 1 teaspoon baking soda
- 1 teaspoon cinnamon
- ½ teaspoon salt
- ¾ cup (180ml) vegetable oil
- 1 cup (340g) honey
- ¾ cup (150g) brown sugar
- 3 eggs
- 1 teaspoon vanilla extract
- 1 cup (240ml) brewed tea or coffee

Instructions:

1. Preheat oven to 350°F (175°C). Grease a 9-inch cake pan.
2. Whisk flour, baking powder, baking soda, cinnamon, and salt.
3. Beat oil, honey, sugar, eggs, and vanilla. Stir in flour mixture and tea/coffee.
4. Bake for 40-45 minutes.

Spice Cake with Brown Butter Frosting

Ingredients:

- 2 ½ cups (315g) all-purpose flour
- 1 teaspoon baking soda
- 1 teaspoon cinnamon
- ½ teaspoon nutmeg
- ½ teaspoon cloves
- ½ teaspoon salt
- ¾ cup (170g) butter, softened
- 1 ½ cups (300g) brown sugar
- 3 eggs
- 1 teaspoon vanilla extract
- 1 cup (240ml) buttermilk

For the frosting:

- ½ cup (113g) butter
- 3 cups (360g) powdered sugar
- ¼ cup (60ml) milk
- 1 teaspoon vanilla extract

Instructions:

1. Preheat oven to 350°F (175°C). Grease two 9-inch cake pans.
2. Beat butter and sugar, then add eggs and vanilla.
3. Mix in dry ingredients and buttermilk.
4. Bake for 30-35 minutes.
5. To make frosting, brown butter in a pan until golden. Cool, then beat with powdered sugar, milk, and vanilla.

Mocha Layer Cake

Ingredients:

- 2 cups (250g) all-purpose flour
- ¾ cup (75g) cocoa powder
- 2 teaspoons baking powder
- ½ teaspoon salt
- 1 cup (200g) sugar
- ¾ cup (180ml) vegetable oil
- 3 eggs
- 1 teaspoon vanilla extract
- ¾ cup (180ml) buttermilk
- ½ cup (120ml) strong brewed coffee

Instructions:

1. Preheat oven to 350°F (175°C). Grease two 9-inch cake pans.
2. Whisk dry ingredients. Beat sugar, oil, eggs, and vanilla.
3. Mix in dry ingredients, buttermilk, and coffee.
4. Bake for 30-35 minutes. Frost with mocha buttercream.

Almond Amaretto Cake

Ingredients:

- 2 ½ cups (315g) all-purpose flour
- 2 teaspoons baking powder
- ½ teaspoon salt
- ¾ cup (170g) butter, softened
- 1 ¾ cups (350g) sugar
- 4 eggs
- 1 teaspoon almond extract
- ¼ cup (60ml) amaretto liqueur
- 1 cup (240ml) milk
- ½ cup (60g) sliced almonds

Instructions:

1. Preheat oven to 350°F (175°C). Grease two 9-inch cake pans.
2. Beat butter and sugar, then add eggs, almond extract, and amaretto.
3. Mix in dry ingredients and milk.
4. Bake for 30-35 minutes. Garnish with sliced almonds.

Sour Cream Coffee Cake

Ingredients:
For the cake:

- 2 cups (250g) all-purpose flour
- 1 teaspoon baking powder
- ½ teaspoon baking soda
- ½ teaspoon salt
- ¾ cup (170g) butter, softened
- 1 cup (200g) sugar
- 2 eggs
- 1 teaspoon vanilla extract
- 1 cup (240g) sour cream

For the cinnamon streusel:

- ½ cup (100g) brown sugar
- 2 teaspoons cinnamon
- ½ cup (60g) chopped walnuts (optional)

Instructions:

1. Preheat oven to 350°F (175°C). Grease a 9-inch bundt pan.
2. Beat butter and sugar, add eggs and vanilla. Mix in dry ingredients and sour cream.
3. Layer half of the batter, sprinkle streusel, then add remaining batter.
4. Bake for 40-45 minutes. Cool and dust with powdered sugar.

Coconut Tres Leches Cake

Ingredients:

For the cake:

- 1 cup (125g) all-purpose flour
- 1 teaspoon baking powder
- ¼ teaspoon salt
- 5 eggs, separated
- 1 cup (200g) sugar
- 1 teaspoon vanilla extract
- ⅓ cup (80ml) whole milk

For the coconut milk mixture:

- 1 can (12 oz) evaporated milk
- 1 can (14 oz) sweetened condensed milk
- ½ cup (120ml) coconut milk

For the topping:

- 1 cup (240ml) heavy whipping cream
- 2 tablespoons sugar
- ½ cup (40g) shredded coconut, toasted

Instructions:

1. Preheat oven to 350°F (175°C). Grease a 9x13-inch pan.
2. Beat egg yolks and sugar, then mix in vanilla and milk. Fold in flour mixture.
3. Beat egg whites until stiff, then fold into batter.
4. Bake for 30 minutes. Poke holes and pour coconut milk mixture over the cake.
5. Chill for 4+ hours, then top with whipped cream and toasted coconut.

Sticky Toffee Pudding Cake

Ingredients:

- 1 cup (175g) chopped dates
- ¾ cup (180ml) boiling water
- 1 teaspoon baking soda
- ½ cup (113g) butter, softened
- ¾ cup (150g) brown sugar
- 2 eggs
- 1 teaspoon vanilla extract
- 1 ½ cups (190g) all-purpose flour
- 1 teaspoon baking powder

For the toffee sauce:

- ½ cup (113g) butter
- 1 cup (200g) brown sugar
- ¾ cup (180ml) heavy cream

Instructions:

1. Preheat oven to 350°F (175°C). Grease a 9-inch cake pan.
2. Soak dates in boiling water and mix in baking soda.
3. Beat butter and sugar, add eggs and vanilla. Stir in flour and baking powder, then fold in dates.
4. Bake for 30-35 minutes.
5. For sauce, heat butter, sugar, and cream until smooth. Pour over warm cake.

Chocolate Peanut Butter Cake

Ingredients:

For the cake:

- 2 cups (250g) all-purpose flour
- ¾ cup (75g) cocoa powder
- 2 teaspoons baking powder
- ½ teaspoon salt
- 1 cup (200g) sugar
- ¾ cup (180ml) vegetable oil
- 3 eggs
- 1 teaspoon vanilla extract
- ¾ cup (180ml) buttermilk
- ½ cup (120ml) hot coffee

For the peanut butter frosting:

- 1 cup (250g) peanut butter
- ½ cup (113g) butter, softened
- 2 cups (240g) powdered sugar
- ¼ cup (60ml) heavy cream

Instructions:

1. Preheat oven to 350°F (175°C). Grease two 9-inch cake pans.
2. Beat sugar, oil, eggs, and vanilla. Mix in dry ingredients, buttermilk, and coffee.
3. Bake for 30-35 minutes.
4. For frosting, beat peanut butter, butter, powdered sugar, and cream. Frost cooled cakes.

Apple Cinnamon Cake

Ingredients:

- 2 cups (250g) all-purpose flour
- 1 teaspoon baking powder
- ½ teaspoon salt
- 1 teaspoon cinnamon
- ½ teaspoon nutmeg
- ¾ cup (170g) butter, softened
- 1 cup (200g) sugar
- 2 eggs
- 1 teaspoon vanilla extract
- 2 apples, peeled and chopped

Instructions:

1. Preheat oven to 350°F (175°C). Grease a 9-inch cake pan.
2. Beat butter and sugar, add eggs and vanilla. Mix in dry ingredients, then fold in apples.
3. Bake for 35-40 minutes.

Chocolate Swiss Roll Cake

Ingredients:

For the cake:

- ¾ cup (90g) all-purpose flour
- ¼ cup (30g) cocoa powder
- 1 teaspoon baking powder
- ½ teaspoon salt
- 4 eggs
- ¾ cup (150g) sugar
- 1 teaspoon vanilla extract

For the filling:

- 1 cup (240ml) heavy whipping cream
- ¼ cup (30g) powdered sugar
- 1 teaspoon vanilla extract

Instructions:

1. Preheat oven to 375°F (190°C). Line a jelly roll pan with parchment paper.
2. Beat eggs and sugar until fluffy, then mix in vanilla. Fold in dry ingredients.
3. Spread batter in pan and bake for 10-12 minutes.
4. Turn onto a towel dusted with powdered sugar and roll while warm.
5. Beat cream, powdered sugar, and vanilla for the filling. Unroll cake, spread filling, then roll back.

www.ingramcontent.com/pod-product-compliance
Lightning Source LLC
LaVergne TN
LVHW081333060526
838201LV00055B/2621